Mexico City:

Out & About

MEXICO CITY:

Out & About

Kenneth and Karen Basile

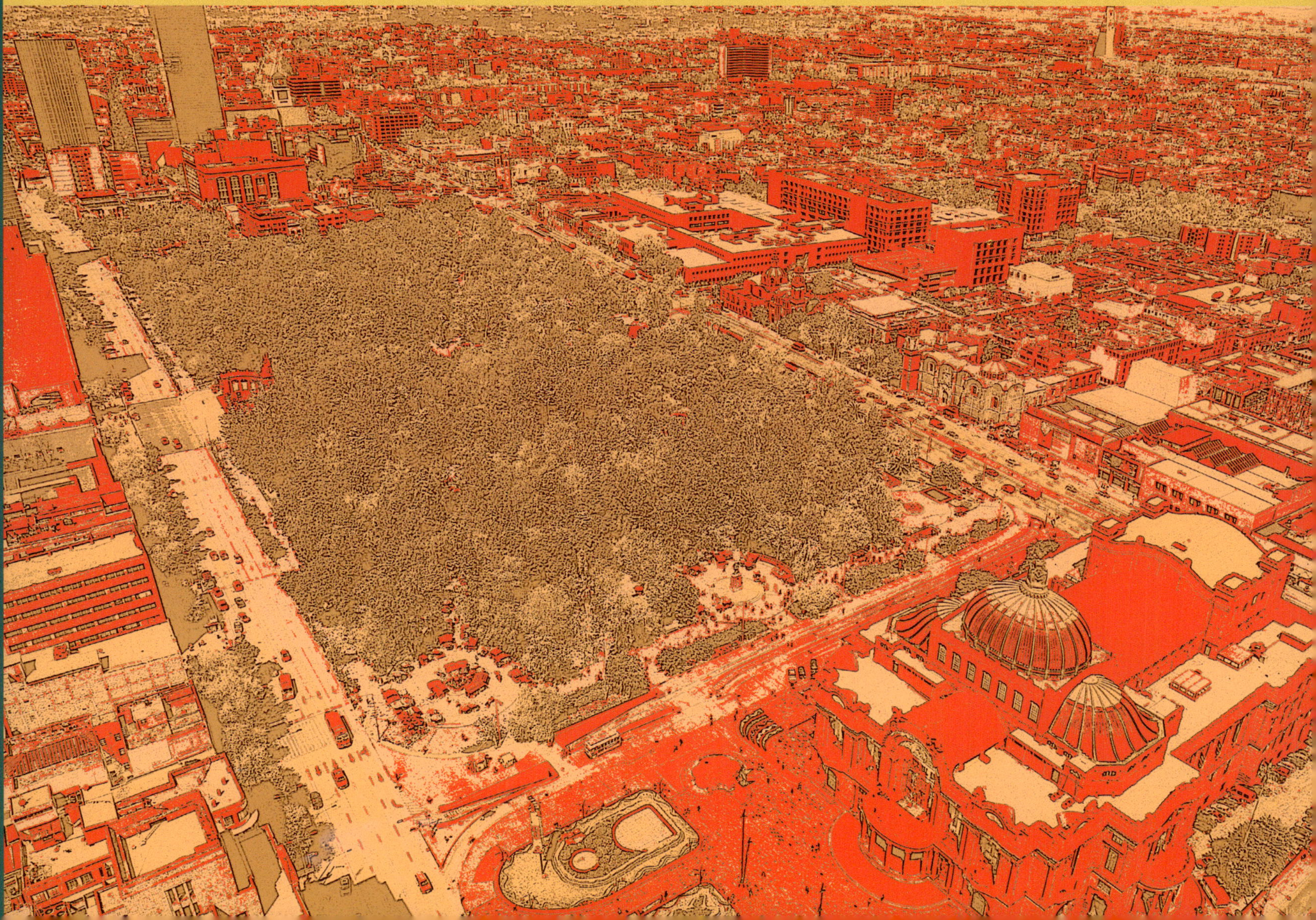

Schiffer Publishing Ltd

4880 Lower Valley Road · Atglen, Pennsylvania 19310

Other Schiffer Books By The Author:
Contemporary Bird Carvings: Two Generations of Bird Carvers, *978-0-7643-2501-9, $49.95*

Other Schiffer Books on Related Subjects:
Maine: Out & About, **978-0-7643-3492-4, $39.99**
Chester County: Out & About, **978-0-7643-3625-6, $45.00**

Library of Congress Control Number: 2010938539

Designed by RoS
Type set in Trajan Pro/Garamond Premier Pro
ISBN: 978-0-7643-3672-0

Printed in Hong Kong

Schiffer Books are available at special discounts for bulk purchases for sales promotions or premiums. Special editions, including personalized covers, corporate imprints, and excerpts can be created in large quantities for special needs. For more information contact the publisher:

Published by Schiffer Publishing Ltd.
4880 Lower Valley Road
Atglen, PA 19310
Phone: (610) 593-1777; Fax: (610) 593-2002
E-mail: Info@schifferbooks.com

For the largest selection of fine reference books on this and related subjects, please visit our web site at **www.schifferbooks.com**
We are always looking for people to write books on new and related subjects. If you have an idea for a book please contact us at the above address.

This book may be purchased from the publisher.
Include $5.00 for shipping.
Please try your bookstore first.
You may write for a free catalog.

In Europe, Schiffer books are distributed by
Bushwood Books
6 Marksbury Ave.
Kew Gardens
Surrey TW9 4JF England
Phone: 44 (0) 20 8392 8585; Fax: 44 (0) 20 8392 9876
E-mail: info@bushwoodbooks.co.uk
Website: www.bushwoodbooks.co.uk

Contents

Acknowledgements

Muchas gracias for their encouragement and assistance to Max Zaragosa; Birger Grinneby; Ana Maria Aragones; our "Mexican family": Arturo, Patti, Elvis, and Claudia Castillo and their families; Gabriel Otero; Helen Escobedo; Salvador Rueda Smithers; Alfredo Hernàndez; Victor and Julio Peña; Angela Espinosa Fuentes; Enrique Osorios; Brenda Lopez; Julia Morales Rosales; Josè Abraham Trejo Henriquez; Alexandra Sanchez Benitez and family; Señor Librarian, Edmundo Garcìa Crisanto, and the security staff at the Benjamin Franklin Library in Mexico City; Richard Newman; Jean Anderton; and the Schiffer family.

Dedicated to our family.

Introduction

TO MEXICO CITY

VITAL, WARM, AND SURREAL, this city is one of the largest in the world and one of the oldest continually inhabited cities in the Western Hemisphere. *El clima*, or the climate, makes it possible and common for citizens of the Distrito Federal, better known as *Defeños*, to be outside every day on the streets and in the parks made for crowds. Warm, sunny afternoons and cool nights year round create the perfect environment for intensely colored flowers, plants, and trees. The warmth in the air is reflected by its people, who are friendly and fun-loving. Andrè Bretòn, the French poet, described Mexico as, "...the surrealist country par excellence." No one seems particularly surprised to see a young woman in a cockroach costume at a subway/bus stop or a woman with angel wings walking in the midst of a crowd on the Zócalo, the large public square. One day the stoplight changes and a contingent of protesting Indians from Veracruz begin to dance naked at the busiest intersection in town. Important historical, anthropological, and art collections, as well as significant musical and theater venues, give the city sophistication on top of a fascinating religious syncretism—a combination of indigenous and Catholic beliefs and customs.

Codices, or Aztec hieroglyphic books, show cartoon-like priests with big heads and short legs carrying religious icons on their backs from place to place. Today it is acceptable to walk around the city carrying a two-foot-tall statue of St. Jude, the Virgin of Guadalupe, or a favorite saint. When the Spanish arrived, they were way outnumbered by the indigenous people. Missionaries found it easiest to convert them to Catholicism by allowing many of the old customs and changing the names of the Aztec gods to saints' names. Anywhere you travel in Mexico, it becomes rapidly clear that the Spanish never erased the Indian presence. Indians wore masks and became the animal or being the mask depicted. Now, one can buy an old mask or reproduction in a gift shop and vendors sell hundreds of *luchador* masks, like those worn by Mexican wrestlers, on the streets in every section of the city. Many traditional dances are still performed using elaborate masks and costumes.

The Mexican version of reality is dreamlike and the attitude toward death affects everyday life, as well as religious ceremony. The belief that the dead inhabit a parallel universe to the one in which we live is made concrete in the Days of the Dead, October 31-November 2. Mexicans traditionally create altars with photos of deceased relatives and place their favorite food and drink to welcome them back for a visit. Candles and bright orange and

red flowers embellish graveyards all over the country, where people sit in vigils waiting to commune with their relatives. Sugar skulls resemble those the Aztec sculpted in their temples and special sweet bread is baked to entice the dead to visit. This holiday is one of several that combine Aztec culture with Catholicism.

Along with the traditional Christmas and Easter, another important religious holiday is Candlemas, February 2, when wooden, ceramic, or plastic dolls representing *Niñopan*, or the Christ Child, are taken to church to be blessed by the priest. In Christianity this date is recognized as the date when baby Jesus was first taken to the temple. Weeks before the holiday, advertisements in the market announce, "We dress Niños." Women busily stitch up fancy costumes for the dolls and sell little gold sandals. All over the city, men, women, and children cradle their family icons in their new outfits and hold them lovingly through mass at the neighborhood church. They return home to altars which usually include a statue of the Virgin of Guadalupe. *La Morena*, or brown-skinned woman, is Mexico's special manifestation of the Virgin Mary and she is everywhere in this city that is 90% Catholic. (See Basílica de Guadalupe on page 146 for her story.)

If you are lucky enough to visit Mexico City, it won't take long to feel the sense of its surreal existence. Exploring the city is easy using a map from one of the tourism kiosks on the Zócalo, the main square of the city, or Chapultepec Park. There are also neighborhood maps and subway maps at each subway stop. The Metro, or subway, is very inexpensive and will take you almost anywhere in the city. The city is organized into *delegaciones*, or city boroughs, and within these are 350 *colonias*, or neighborhoods. The vast city of more than 20 million people seems overwhelming, but the areas of interest are easily located. People everywhere are friendly and helpful. Traveling by motor vehicle is slow and taxis with the proper licensing are recommended and inexpensive. Be aware that one doesn't need to take a test to get a driver's license and driving in one of the largest cities in the world can be nerve wracking.

If you visit, you'll want to return.

SCRATCH THE SURFACE anywhere in Mexico City and you will find pre-Columbian remains. Remnants of various Indian civilizations sit below the surface throughout the Valley of Mexico. In fact, the first Christian church in Mexico, now known as the Metropolitan Cathedral, was built using stones the Spanish took from the temple in the center of Tenochtitlán, as Mexico City was known at the time of the Spanish conquest in 1520.The Mexica Indians founded Tenochtitlán on an island in the midst of Lake Texcoco in 1325. But as early as 1200 B.C. there were different groups of up to 20,000 indigenous people living in what are now the southern suburbs. Volcanic eruptions sent them toward the north. Nomads from the west and north were later led by their priests into the valley to the present site of Mexico City. The Mexica settled on an island in the shallow lake that filled the valley and the population of the valley grew to over one million by the time the Spanish arrived. There were hundreds of temple complexes. The Templo Mayor, or Main Temple, was where the city's main square, or Zócalo, is today. In 1502 the Spanish entered a city larger than any that existed in Spain at the time. The civilization was complex, with a written language, system of government, organized religion, water systems, sophisticated agricultural techniques, an accurate calendar, libraries, and schools.

The unearthing of sites of these great civilizations is fairly recent. The Templo Mayor was uncovered as recently as 1978, when new electrical cables were being laid. As the city spread and super highways and the subway were expanded, fragments of the ancient Aztec civilizations came to light. Aztec is a generic name for the many different Indians who speak a form of Nàhuatl.

It is interesting to observe the Indian influence on the surface culture, as well. Mexican Spanish consists of hundreds of words that are not Castilian but originate from Indian dialects. In fact, more than 130,000 people living in Mexico City still speak an Indian dialect. Names of subway stops alone give one a clue about the pervasive influence of Indian culture in the big city: Tacuba, Xochimilco, Tacubaya, Xola, Nezahualpilli, Tepepan, Huichapan, Coyoacán, Mixcoac, Iztacalco...

The Aztec City
This mural by Miguel Covarrubias in the National Museum of Anthropology shows Tenochtitlán, as Mexico City was called by the Mexica Indians who were living there when Cortès arrived in 1519. Causeways led out to other Indian villages in the valley.

ARCHAEOLOGICAL SITES

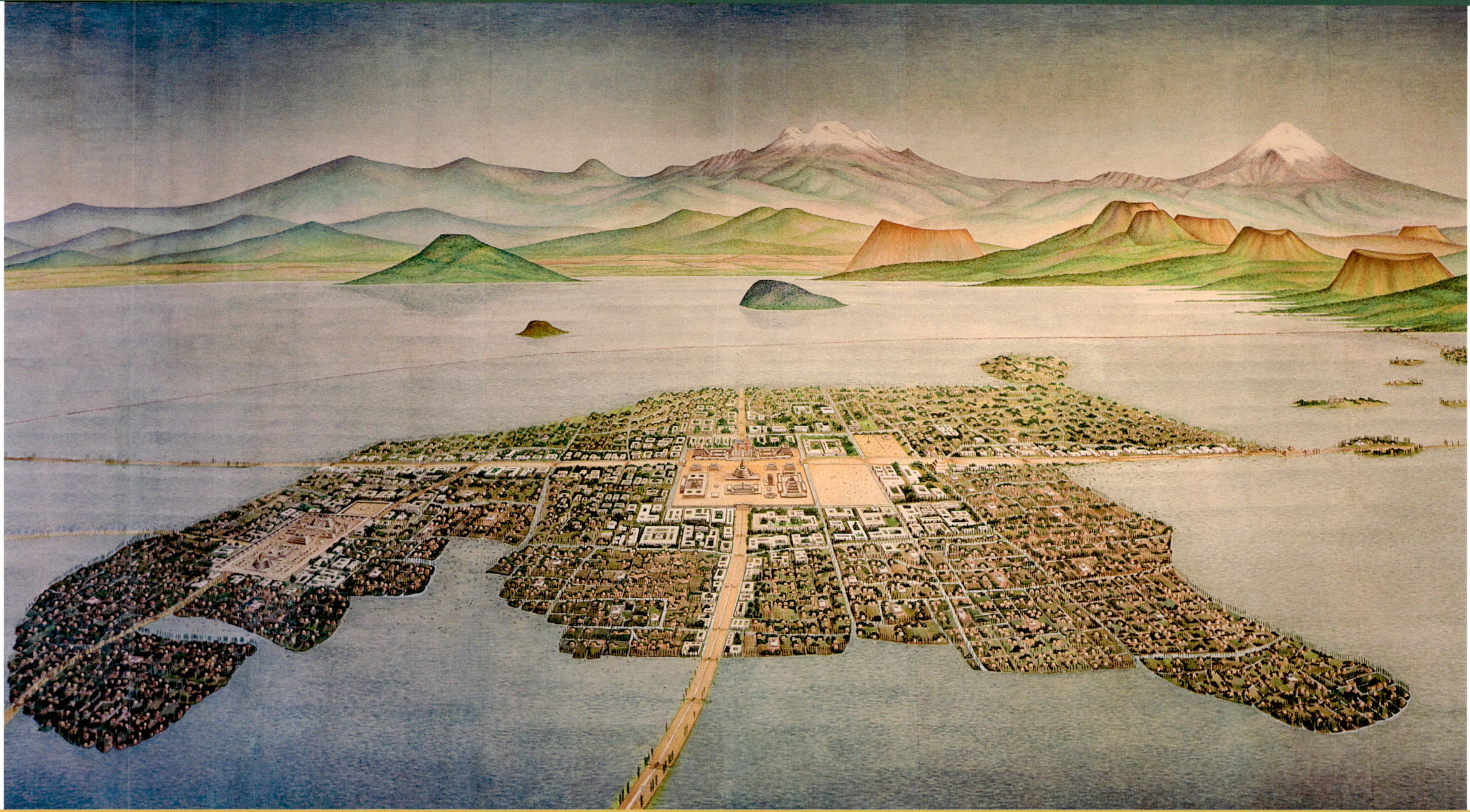

Opposite:

Templo Mayor Ruins

The remains of the Mexica Indians' Templo Mayor stand next to the National Cathedral and the National Palace on the Zócalo, or main square. An excellent museum is on site. [Exit the Metro at Zócalo and walk north one block.]

Skull Over Font

A skull similar to the ones on Aztec altars watches over a holy water font in the church of San Bernadino in Xochimilco, a southern neighborhood of Mexico City. Náhuatl for "Place Where Flowers are Grown," Xochimilco is often symbolized by the flower motif. [See page 164.]

Skull Platform

Many Aztec ruins include platforms on which skulls of enemies were displayed, especially near ancient courts where Tlachtli, an Aztec ball game, was played. This Tzompantli Altar in the Templo Mayor ruins is covered with 240 stone skulls. It was a part of an altar that may have been used for sacrifices.

Opposite:

Subway Ruins

In 1967, during construction of line two of the subway, ruins of a temple to the Aztec wind god, Ehècatl, were unearthed. Inside was a stone box containing shells, pottery, and a small statue of a dancing monkey with a duck bill, a typical wind god icon. [View underground at Pino Saurez Metro station.]

Clockwise from top:

Palatial Cats

Resident cats have taken over these colonial remains on the back patio of the National Palace. [On the Zócalo]

Tlatelolco

The ceremonial center here was very similar to the one in Tenochtitlán. During the 1990s, fifty-four burial offerings were found in forty-one graves and the archaeological find is still being interpreted. Remains extend under the nearby streets and buildings.

Three Culture Ruins

Pre-Columbian Aztec ruins in the Tlatelolco neighborhood are still being excavated. A colonial church, with its convent and twentieth century apartment buildings, are visible in the background. These three buildings from different time periods give the square its name, the Plaza of Three Cultures. [Exit Tlatelolco Metro and walk north three blocks.]

Pyramid at Tlatelolco
Reconstruction of the pyramids and altars at this village, which was northeast of Tenochtitlán, is ongoing.

Opposite:
Aqueduct
Part of the water aqueduct that ran from a spring at Chapultepec Park to the center of the city has been preserved along Chapultepec Avenue. The system was begun in 1620 and completed in the eighteenth century. [Chapultepec Avenue, two blocks north of Sevilla Metro exit]

Cincalco
The Aztecs believed the cave at the base of the hill where Chapultepec Castle now sits was the entrance to the underworld. [In Chapultepec Park in the Audiorama. See page 63 and 64.]

Salto del Agua Fountain
One of the last remaining fountains that delivered water from the aqueducts, this one, completed in 1716, now sits in the midst of a busy intersection and just past the Salto del Agua, or Fountain of Water subway stop. [One block east of Salto de Agua Metro stop]

CYNESA

Olmec Tomb
This tomb replica, located in the gardens of the National Museum of Anthropology in Chapultepec Park, has a Grecian style cornice. The Olmec lived in the Valley of Mexico from 1200-400 B.C. They are said to be the mother culture of all Mexican Indians. [In Chapultepec Park]

Hundido Park
Hundido, or "Big Hole," Park has an interesting array of reproduction, pre-Columbian sculptures arranged by time period. This is a copy of an ancient Olmec head. [Metrobus stop Parque Hundido]

Cuicuilco Temple
Some of the oldest pre-Columbian remains in the southern part of the city are surrounded by the busy beltway and another major artery. Living here from 700-100 B.C., the 20,000 inhabitants fled north toward Tlateloco after volcanic eruptions. Cuicuilco means, "Place of Song and Dance," and the circular form suggests association with the wind god. [Metrobus to Villa Olimpica]

Mixcoac Fountain
The Mixcoac neighborhood takes its name from Náhuatl and means, "Serpent of the Clouds." This god was worshipped in the southeastern area of the city during pre-Columbian times and the remains of a temple dedicated to the serpent god are nearby. [Taxi to Mixcoac]

Mixcoac Temple
These remains of a temple to the Serpent of the Clouds lie next to the busy beltway. [Taxi. This temple may not be open to the public.]

Opposite:

Salute to the Sun

The pyramid at Cuicuilco is a popular spot for meditation and large groups converge on it and other temple sites for solstice and equinox celebrations.

Olympic Remains

The 1968 Olympic playing fields are now part of a sports club. Some of the remains of the Cuicuilco culture were unearthed and partially destroyed during the construction of the fields.

Cerro de Las Estrellas

"Hill of the Stars," this 8000 foot high temple was the site of the Old Fire Ceremony, an event the Aztecs held every fifty-two years. Comparable to a century in the modern calendar, change was marked by extinguishing all fires. A new fire was built atop this extinct volcano by Aztec priests. The Valley of Mexico is visible for miles on all sides. [Metro to Cerro de las Estrellas; taxi up the hill, then walk to top]

[Metro to Zócalo: most of the sites are within a three block walk of the main square. Pedicabs are available.]

THE HISTORIC DISTRICT

CENTRO HISTORICO, AS IT IS KNOWN, is truly the historic center of one of the oldest cities in the Western Hemisphere. Aztecs settled here in 1325 following a prophecy sent from the gods, in which they were advised to build a city where an eagle perched on a cactus devoured a snake. Written Indian codices, or hieroglyphic books, in the Anthropology Museum in Chapultepec Park attest to this history and this image is centered on the red, white, and green Mexican flag today. At that time, Tenochtitlán, as it was called, became a thriving Aztec city in the middle of a shallow lake. The Spanish conquistadores ripped apart the large Aztec temple and its stones were used to build the elaborate Metropolitan Cathedral, which is today the center of the Catholic Church in Latin America. Since the Aztec emperor Montezuma's time, the area has been the center of church and state and its square is faced with the National Palace and important Aztec ruins, as well as the cathedral. Called the Zócalo, the Plaza of the Constitution in the center is the largest public space next to Red Square in Moscow. Its name means pedestal in Spanish. President Santa Ana erected a pedestal there in 1840 to hold a proposed monument. Although the monument was never built, the name stuck and Zócalo is used throughout the country to identify town squares. Independence celebrations, Days of the Dead events, a winter wonderland with ice skating rink, spring fiestas, book fairs, protest marches, and Aztec dancers—there is always something happening around the giant Mexican flag in the center of the Zócalo. Fanning out in all directions from this vast public square are more plazas with fascinating histories, museums, colonial mansions, monuments, an elaborate concert hall, some of the best shopping, and a 44-story modern building with a viewing platform on top. Some of Mexico City's oldest treasures are centered here.

Fountain Wreath
At the Ministry of Finance Museum on Moneda Street, roses, lilies, babies' breath (Gypsofilia) and ferns fill a fountain in the center of the courtyard.

The National Palace
The Federal Government meets in the National Palace on Plaza de la Constituciòn, commonly known as the Zócalo.

Unemployed
Just off the Zócalo, unemployed men advertise their trades: electrical, tile work, painting, and plumbing. The Metropolitan Cathedral is behind them.

Demonstration
Protest workers are often seen on the streets of the historic district around the Zócalo where the government offices are. This demonstration against the ruling conservative party held up traffic for most of the day.

Popular Front
Living in tents pitched between the Zócalo and Santo Domingo Square, demonstrators camp out for days and march against the government.

Invierno en la Capital

ITALIA
Clorets

Opposite, clockwise from top:

Santos for Sale
Shops selling religious statues and botanicals line a shopping passageway behind the Metropolitan Cathedral on the Zócalo.

Skating Rink
People stand in line for hours in order to experience ice skating, sledding, and making a snowman on the Zócalo from the end of November until early January. Keeping the ice and snow frozen requires huge amounts of energy in the 75°F weather.

Christmas on the Zócalo
Landscape designs around the square and lighted displays on the sides of the buildings fronting the Zócalo change with the seasons.

Subway Stairs
El Metro, the city's subway system, is always busy. It is an inexpensive way to travel just about anywhere in the city quickly. This crowd is approaching and leaving the Zócalo.

Catrinas
At the turn of the nineteenth century, cartoonist Jose Guadalupe Posadas created a well-dressed lady skeleton named Catrina who wore a fancy hat. Today you see her all over the country during the festivities of the Days of the Dead. Altars cover the Zócalo for weeks before and after the Days of the Dead, October 31 to November 2.

Besame Mucho
On February 14, 2009, the city broke the Guinness World Records for the most people kissing at one time, with 39,897 smoochers in the Zócalo.

Opposite, clockwise from top:

Breakdancers
There is always some form of street entertainment happening around the Zócalo.

Traditional Healer
On most days near the Metropolitan Cathedral a "cleansing" can be bought from an Indian *curandero* who burns copal incense and herbs to cure illness and to dispel negative forces.

Plaza de Santo Domingo
Doña Josefa Ortiz sits above the square. She is honored there because in 1810, when she was the mayor's wife, she warned Miguel Hidalgo's revolutionary forces that they were about to be arrested by the viceregal army.

Beggar
Beggars stake out territory in busy spots all over the city. This one sits in front of the cathedral.

Portal de las Evangelistas
A couple waits while a hand-printed invitation is made to order. The arcade facing Plaza de Santo Domingo has been a traditional gathering place for scribes since the 1400s.

Alameda Park and Palace
From the 44th floor of the Latin American Tower, The Palacio de Belles Artes and Alameda Park are visible, just a few blocks from the Zócalo.

Clockwise from top:

Benito Juarez Monument
The semicircular monument to Benito Juàrez, president of Mexico from 1858-1872, fans out from the edge of the Alameda.

Courtyard Gallery
The courtyard between the Latin American Tower and the Temple of San Francisco and Chapel of Balvenera displays contemporary sculpture. Angela Guerrìa's *Disk of Butterflies* is in the foreground. Butterflies and jaguars are traditional Aztec themes.

Romance in the Park
Lovers are not shy about using the parks all over the city for romance. This couple is in the busy Alameda.

Mounted Police
The Alameda is patrolled by special mounted police who wear traditional sombreros and uniforms.

Monument to Mexican Nationality
A prophetic eagle devouring a snake on a cactus was the sign to the Mexica Indians that they should build a city on the island in the middle of the valley. This monument by Juan Olaguìbel stands opposite the Supreme Court. Marigolds (Calendula) are planted for the fall season.

Opposite:
Museum Courtyard
The interior courtyard of the Ministry of Finance Museum displays sculpture by Francisco Zuñiga.

Tolsà Square
The statue of King Charles IV of Spain (1788-1808), was placed in this square in front of the National Art Museum in 1979. Dressed as a Roman soldier, he has moved from his original site on Paseo de la Reforma, replaced by the large, modern *Caballito* by Sebastiàn at the beginning of the Reforma. Prior to his placement on the Reforma, King Charles presided over the Zócalo.

Opposite:

Museum Patio

The patio of the Franz Mayer Museum features an unusual Telavera tile fountain shaped like a compass rose surrounded by boxwood (Buxus microphylla) trees and azalea (Ericaceae).

Convent Plaza

In the plaza of the Convent of the Merced, Alonzo Garcia navigates his way through the vendors of CDs and clothing. Garcia, accompanied by two Aztecs, drew up the first map of Mexico City.

Garibaldi Plaza

In this large open plaza, one can pay to be serenaded by traditional mariachi bands.

Clockwise from top:

Dolls for Sale
Dolls, often with handmade clothing, are sold in many of the markets and plazas of the city.

Niños for Sale
Vendors selling baby Christ figures are a common sight before Christmas, Candlemas, and other religious holidays. Next to the niños, medicinal herbs are for sale.

Convent of Tlatelolco
This Franciscan monastery, begun in 1530, was the setting for the writings of Father Bernadino de Sahagun who wrote twelve volumes of *A General History of New Spain*. [Metro to Tlatelolco, north three blocks]

Opposite:

Santiago Garden
At the time of the Spanish conquest, this block was occupied by a large indigenous market. The symmetrical park features four cement gates and a pavilion today. [Metro to Tlatelolco, north two blocks]

[Start at the Plaza de la Republica east to the *Caballito*, then walk southwest. The best way to see this seven mile stretch of road is to take a tour on the Turibus, which stops at several places in the city. A good place to start is the Zócalo. This allows you to disembark and spend time at each landmark.]

PASEO DE LA REFORMA, a seven-and-one-half-mile-long, eight-lane corridor bisecting the ancient heart of the city, was originally conceived in 1864 by Emperor Maximilian as a Mexican Champs Elysées. Known then as the Emperor's Walk, it stretched from the castle in Chapultepec, where he resided, to the National Palace on the Plaza de la Constitucièn, or Zócalo, where the government has convened since. In 1867 the name was changed to Paseo de la Reforma to honor the Reform Laws of 1867. During the Reform, laws under the government of Benito Juarez seized church property and public education was made mandatory. Thirty-eight statues of renowned reformers from around the country stand on either side of the wide boulevard. Six *glorietas*, or traffic circles, serve as display points for five iconic sculptures and one very tall palm tree. The Angel, a statue of Winged Victory, has become a symbol for the city and an important gathering spot. She stands atop the 118-foot-tall Column of Independence. The monument was based on a design by Antonio Rivas Mercado and built by Roberto Gayol, with sculptures by Enrique Alciati. If there is going to be a city celebration, it will probably be near the Angel or on the Zócalo. The eight center lanes of the Reforma are often barricaded for several blocks for parades, bicycling, or other special events. Four lanes along the side allow traffic to continue moving, albeit slowly. Wide sidewalks with benches and gardens lining the edges and through the middle make the street a pleasant place to stroll—periodic exhibits and events are staged there. Tall, modern glass buildings are replacing historic homes that once were a sign of wealth in the city. The present Reforma stretches from one end of the modern city to the southern beltway, or Periferico. A typical weekend finds the Reforma blocked off for family events.

The Angel
The gilded symbol of the city, the 105-foot-tall landmark represents Winged Victory. Sculpted by Enrique Alciati, she blesses the city atop the Column of Independence. Around the base are heroes of the Mexican War of Independence from Spain and female figures representing war, peace, justice, and law. The remains of twelve heroes of the revolution are in the base.

PASEO DE LA REFORMA

Puerta 1808
Door 1808 is a 2007 abstract addition dedicated to the independence movement from Spain in 1808. It was created by Manuel Felguerez and sits across from the *Caballito*.

Caballito
The *Little Horse*, a 65-foot-tall sculpture designed by Enrique Carvajal Gonzàlez, known as Sebastiàn, replaced the statue of Charles IV of Spain after it was moved to the square in front of the National Museum of Art. *Caballito* marks the beginning of the Reforma.

Opposite:
St. Jude Altar
In San Fernando Plaza an altar to St. Jude, patron saint of lost causes, provides solace to the homeless who live in the plaza.

National Lottery Building
This fanciful art deco building sits at the traffic circle at the beginning of the Reforma. Mexico has had a national lottery since 1770.

Monument to the Mexican Revolution
Revolutionary leaders' remains rest in this monument along with a Museum of the Revolution. Located in the Plaza of the Republic, just off the Reforma, the structure was begun as a legislative palace but building was interrupted by the war in 1910. Architect Carlos Obregòn Santacilla designed it.

Staple Bench
Appearing like giant staples, this is one of many benches commissioned by the government in the early twenty-first century to grace the Reforma's wide central walkways.

Francisco Zarco
Zarco orates in the San Fernanado Plaza. The statue was erected to honor him and other journalists who "always tell the truth." Homeless people and a dog sleep like cocoons in front of his statue.

Jose Reyes Heroles Park
A leaf sculpture dedicated to L. Ron Hubbard, founder of Scientology, is reflected in one of the modern buildings at the busy intersection of la Reforma and Insurgentes Avenue.

Opposite:

La Banca Baraja

Playing cards fall to the sidewalk in Brian Nissen's 2006 sculptured bench, *The Deck Bench.*

Clockwise from top:

Dr. Rafael Lucio

This is one of thirty-six monuments along the Reforma that honor people who were active in the Reform movement throughout Mexico. Dr. Lucio was a pediatrician.

Cuauhtèmoc Monument

As the last Aztec leader to fight Cortès after Montezuma was killed, Cuauhtèmoc is honored throughout the city. The base of the monument on the Reforma lists the four other tribal leaders who fought the Spaniards. Cortès took Cuauhtèmoc to Honduras where he hanged him. Manuel Noreña sculpted this piece in 1884.

Columbus Monument

Columbus gestures toward the horizon in this statue created by Charles Cordier in Paris and given to the city by Don Antonio Escandòn in 1877. Seated around his feet are various friars who supported the education of Indians in Mexico.

Clockwise from top:

Cuauhtèmoc Bas Relief

Cuauhtèmoc and a fellow warrior are literally having their feet held to the fire in this frieze on the side of his monument. Cortès tortured the Indians to try to find the location of their gold treasure. Bas reliefs on all four sides are by Gabriel Guerría.

Reformer with Bench

Pedro Mendez, one of the Reformers, seems to be holding the upside down man on the bench behind him by a string.

Reforma Bench

A bench created in 2003 for the Reforma renewal program sits near the Column of Independence.

Sit Here
These benches, designed by Naomi Siegmand in 2006, are called *Sit in Your House.*

"Veracruz 400" Protest
Men move into the street while women dance naked in front of drums being played. The nudity is meant to demonstrate that they have nothing left. The signs indicate that the government will not negotiate with the poor farmers from whom land was taken. They camped out at the base of the Monument to Motherhood for over a year and collected donations until spring 2009 when the government of Veracruz opened negotiations.

"Veracruz 400" Protestors
Protestors dance in a busy intersection when traffic is stopped at a red light. They claim the Veracruz state government took their land.

Opposite:

Fallen Angel
During the earthquake of 1957, the angel fell off her pedestal. She was repaired but the smashed head is mounted in the foyer of the Casa de los Condes de Hera y Soto, now a city records building in the Historic District.

Plant Sale
Annual plant markets are set up under awnings on the Reforma before Christmas. Similarly, books are sold here in the fall.

Chinese New Year Parade
The annual Chinese New Year parade in February is popular. The viewing stand is next to the Column of Independence.

Spring Parade
A butterfly on a bike pedals down the Reforma for the Spring Parade. Parents, teachers, and children from various nursery schools participate.

Christmas Scene
A young girl takes a photo with her mother's cell phone. This is one of many Nativity scenes that line the Reforma during the Christmas season.

Advertising on the Reforma
A credit card company changes the view on a mammoth billboard to entice travel.

Palm Tree Glorieta
The very tall palm in the middle of the roundabout at the Reforma and Niza Street is dwarfed by the Mexican Stock Exchange building.

Allium Blooming
Allium (Alliaceae) bloom in the spring around the palm tree glorieta.

Carrington Sculptures
Leonora Carrington's sculptures line the median strip of the Reforma where it bisects Chapultepec Park and is the site of changing exhibitions. Carrington is a well known British surrealist painter and sculptor born in 1917. She spent many years in Mexico and now lives in Mexico City.

Diana Fountain
Presently Diana hunts in the nude, but in the 1940s, conservative government officials made her wear a skirt. Created in 1942, the sculptor was Juan Olaguibel. In the right background is the 52-story Torre Mayor, the tallest building in Latin America.

Pemex Fountain
This fountain, with sculpture by Juan Olaguibel, sits at the Reforma and the Periferico, or beltway, and commemorates the nationalization of all the oil companies in 1938.

[Exit from the Chapultepec Metro station. The park is a good place to pick up a tourist map produced by the Secretary of Tourism. Maps are also posted through the park.]

KNOWN AS EL BOSQUE, or "The Woods," by locals, this park is Mexico City's Central Park. It offers dense landscaping; a zoo; playgrounds; an amusement park; a water park; a senior citizens' center; lakes with paddle boats, kayaks, and rowboats; a botanical garden; bandstands; and seven world class museums. The oldest park in the Americas, it covers 1600 acres and supports 150 species of vegetation, including 300-year-old Mexican Cypress and 150 species of animals. It is well maintained and comfortable for exercising, picnicking, or sightseeing. On weekends the park fills with locals and more than 15 million people visit each year.

Chapultepec Castle guards the park from atop a volcanic hill with a mythological history. Natural springs that were here left evidence of early humans dating back 3250 years. There is magic surrounding the hill where a cave known as Cincalco leads to the underworld, according to Aztec legend. The hill has been the home of powerful leaders since Montezuma lived here and bathed in the pools at its base. Aqueducts were built then to carry water from the hill to Tenochtitlán, as Mexico City was called at the time of Cortés' conquest. In the mid Eighteenth Century, Viceroys Matias and Bernardo de Galvez ordered the construction of the castle as a country retreat. King Maximilian and Queen Carlota of Hapsburg had the castle on the hill restored and landscaped in the mid 1850s, when they lorded over "New Spain," after the French invasion. It was at one time a military academy, then the home of President Porfirio Dìaz for thirty years before the Revolution of 1910. It became a museum in 1935, when President Cardenas moved to other quarters in the park known as Los Pinos. Mexico's president lives in Los Pinos today in a heavily guarded secluded corner of the park and the castle is open to the public.

Grasshopper Symbol
A representation of the Aztec image of a grasshopper on a hill is used as the logo for the park. Chapultepec means "Grasshopper Hill" in Nàhuatl.

Chapultepec is an Náhuatl word meaning "Grasshopper Hill" and its significance is unclear. We know that Aztecs ate grasshoppers for protein (Mexicans still enjoy these crunchy treats). In the Museum of Anthropology there is an old grasshopper effigy carved in red stone that was found near Montezuma's bathing pools. Whatever the meaning of its name, the magic of the park can still be felt.

CHAPULTEPEC PARK

Clockwise from top:

Chapultepec Castle
Seen from atop a nearby building, one senses the placement of the castle atop its hill.

Castle Terrace
All along the terraces of the castle, cement urns are planted with purple lantana (Verbenaceae).

View from the Castle
The view to the north looks over the Monument to Child Heroes to the Avenida de la Reforma. The Angel on her pedestal is visible in the distance.

Child Heroes
Military College cadets defended the Castle against American troops in 1847. Six of them leaped to their deaths rather than surrender. These statues on the terrace memorialize them.

Clockwise from top:

Morning in the Park
People swarm into Chapultepec Park around 10:30 in the morning. Flowering jacaranda trees (Jacaranda mimoifolia) trees in the background and allium in the foreground bask in the sun.

David
David prepares to cast his stone in front of the Fountain of Temperance.

Castle Grounds
Once barren rock, the hill on which the castle sits is now covered with palms and subtropical trees that simulate a jungle.

Garden of the Castle Keep
In the late 1800s, President Porfirio Diaz installed the interior garden with statuary and frescoes related to the woods. They were redesigned in 1999. Manicured boxwood and euonymous set off seasonal plants such as these poinsettia (Euphorbia pulcherrima) in pots.

Music Garden Entrance
The Audiorama is a small open air music garden with comfortable benches. Music is played through speakers mounted in four corners throughout the day.

Clockwise from top:

Audiorama
People relax while they listen to music.

White Edged Aloe
These aloe (Aloeaceae) add variation to the cactus garden.

Cactus Flower
Flowers of the Epiphyllum cooperi bloom in March in the Chapultepec Park cactus garden.

Greenhouse Orchid
The greenhouses in the park contain hundreds of varieties of orchids (Coelogyne) and bromeliads (Bromeliaceae).

Clockwise from top:

Chapultepec Lake

Weekends find this lake full of people in paddle boats and rowboats. The House of the Lake, on the opposite shore, is a cultural center.

National Museum of Anthropology, Exterior Garden

One can walk outside the overwhelming collections and spend time among reproductions of pre-Columbian temples and monuments set in a lush jungle garden.

National Museum of Anthropology, Interior Courtyard

Water falls from the suspended ceiling above the column decorated with Aztec motifs. This striking building was designed by Pedro Vazquez, Jorge Campuzano, Rafael Majeres, and Ricardo de Robina. Its collection makes it one of the most important anthropology museums in the world.

Voladores
Several times a day beside the National Museum of Anthropology, the Totonac Indians perform the fertility rite that was observed once a year in Veracruz. Before climbing the pole, they dance slowly around it to the flute and drum player's rhythm.

Volador
After climbing the pole, the ropes are twisted around it and when the flute player who sits on top stops playing, four *voladores* fall backward and slowly spin until near the ground.

Opposite:
Conchero Dancers
Aztec dancers perform traditional dances and rites near the National Museum of Anthropology and throughout the city.

Poets' Pathway
Manuel Acuna is one of ten Mexican poets memorialized by busts in the park's lovely gardens.

Tamayo Park
The newest section of the park contains trees donated in 1981 by countries from all over the world. It has walking, biking, and running paths.

Sunbather
A visitor enjoys the warm sun on one of the benches near the museums.

Picnic Area
Next to the Tamayo Museum, the metal awning provides shade for picnickers during warm Mexican afternoons.

Clockwise from top:

Old Cypress

The park has about 140 Montezuma Cypress (Pinus montezumae) that are more than 300 years old.

Kaffir Lilies

These 18-inch-tall lilies (Clivia miniata) add color to many of the parks.

Reflecting Pools

These pools planted with papyrus (Cyperus papyrus) were added, along with a walkway, in 2002 to connect the National Museum of Anthropology to the Tamayo Museum.

Clockwise from top:

Chapultepec Zoo
One of three zoos in the city, this is the largest and has a good collection of more than 200 well-cared-for species, including an aviary and butterfly house.

Elephant Ears
Philodendrum domesticum plants are well-tended like the rest of the Garden of the Third Age. The area is put to good use and classes in horticulture, English, and dance are popular.

Museum of Natural History
Consisting of a series of large domes, this museum has exhibits about the body, the universe, evolution, and some dinosaur bones.

Opposite:

Fountain of Tlaloc

Painting and sculpture are combined in this Diego Rivera-designed monument to the Aztec water god Tlaloc. It is located in Section II of Chapultepec Park at the waterworks that receive the water of the Lerma River.

The Cycle of Life

Sculpture such as this one by Lidia Lobation de Dabbah is placed among walking paths and gardens in the Garden of the Third Age, an area of Chapultepec where one has to be over 60 years of age to enter.

Lincoln Park Storyteller
The park is busy with many activities for children on the weekends. [Metro to Auditorio, three blocks north, three blocks west]

A MAP BOOK OF MEXICO CITY lists 153 parks and gardens, 109 plazas, four archaeological sites, and three zoos. In addition, almost every neighborhood has at least one church with an atrium, or large plaza, in front of it. Many museums and monuments are surrounded by large green spaces and small, nicely landscaped pieces of land set into busy streets add color to the vast metropolis. Gardens and landscaped pathways bisect many thoroughfares. In this city of more than twenty million people, it is always possible to find a tranquil bench placed near a burbling fountain, sweet smelling roses, or a shady tree. There is always something blooming with vibrant color and adding sweetness to the crisp smells of street food sold at small stands. The parks and gardens and other public spaces of the city give it special warmth. One never has to walk far to escape the noise of traffic and the bustle of people moving to and from school and work. *Defeños*, as citizens of the Distrito Federal are known, are fond of using their parks. During the afternoon break for *comida*, the midday meal, people meet and congregate in public spaces. Weekends fill the parks with families enjoying the sun and playing. The temperate climate of the city makes outdoor activity possible throughout the year. Strolling, bike riding, playing sports, walking dogs, dancing, sleeping on the soft grass, or just sitting on a bench, the people of Mexico City relish their parks.

Tour Bus
Old busses and cars are kept alive in the city. This one waits beside the Ciudadela Market, a popular craft market. [Metro stop Balderas, three blocks north]

NEIGHBORHOOD PARKS & GARDENS

Kiosk in Santa Marìa de Ribera Park
This cast-iron kiosk in Moorish style was built for the International Exposition in New Orleans in 1884 and later moved to this spot. [Metro stop Buena Vista, three blocks west, one block north]

Moorish Kiosk
Designed by Josè Ramòn de Ibarrola, prior to being moved to its present location in 1908, this kiosk was moved from New Orleans to the Alameda in 1890.

Danzon Park
Sunday afternoons find the Plaza José Marie Morelos y Pavon full of dancers who practice a complex Cuban style of ballroom dancing called Danzon. [Metro stop Balderas, three blocks north]

Couples in Danzon Park
Young and old enjoy the music and movement of the dance.

Opposite:

The "400" Clean Up
Under the Monument to Motherhood statue, a block away from the Reforma, demonstrators who have been camped out for months wash clothes and bathe. They are the "Veracruz 400," who are demonstrating against the state of Veracruz, which they say took their land. The monument was created in the 1950s by Luis Ortiz Monasterio. [Metrobus Insurgentes, three blocks northeast]

Art Park
Sullivan Park, behind the Monument to Motherhood, has long been known as Art Park. On weekends artists display and sell their work. Classes are also held. [Metro Insurgentes, three blocks northeast, one block east]

Radio Park in San Juan Plaza
Francisco Nari Cano (1921-2006) created Radio Broadcasters Day. His is one of several busts that circle the fountain in the middle of San Juan Plaza.

Opposite, clockwise from top:

San Juan Plaza
Ernest Pugibet looks over Ayuntamiento Street, or Town Hall Street. The rotunda behind him is filled with busts of *locutores*, or radio broadcasters, and is funded by the radio broadcasters union. [Metro stop Balderas, three blocks north, four blocks east]

Pushkin Graffiti
Graffiti in Pushkin Garden has even despoiled his bust. Someone has left flowers for him in a styrofoam cup. [Metro stop Cuauhtemoc, four blocks south]

"In Memory of Julio"
A small triangle of trees and amyrllis near a busy subway station contains a cross placed there by friends in memory of Julio.

FAllECIO
SRor JULIO B H
El dia 12 Junio de 1999
Recuerdo de sus
Amigos

Luis Cabrera Plaza

This plaza in the Roma neighborhood is used by students of the nearby school and hospital workers. Pruned amaryllis will be blooming in a couple of months. [Metro stop Insurgentes, one block east, three blocks south]

Blue Wall
Buildings near Pushkin Garden, and all over the city, are painted bright, vibrant colors.

Pushkin Park Graffiti
As in any large city, graffiti, an accepted art form, is found in many of the parks, despite many efforts to stop it.

Guadalupe Shrine
The Virgin of Guadalupe is distinctly Mexican and shrines to her are found everywhere in the city. This one is tucked in at the edge of Pushkin Park. The collection box is for the nearby church.

Popocatèpetl Roundabout
The art deco fountain on the roundabout at Amsterdam Avenue was designed by Josè Gòmez Echeverrìa in 1927. [Sevilla Metro, seven blocks southeast]

Dr. Ignacio Chavez Garden Fountain
Dr. Chavez was a poet, as well as a physician. Streets leading to the west from this park are all named after doctors. [Metro stop Cuauhtemoc, three blocks south]

David on the Plaza
A copy of Michelangelo's David stands in the center of Rio de Janeiro Plaza in the Roma neighborhood. [Insurgentes Metro stop, one block east, two blocks south]

Cibeles Roundabout
A homeless man in the Roma neighborhood drinks from the fountain under *Cibeles*, a reproduction of a fountain in Madrid. Spain gifted the fountain of Jupiter's mother to Mexico. [Metrostop Insurgentes, three blocks southwest]

Mexico Park
Idyllic cement "log" bridges span streams running through this popular park named after General San Martin, but commonly known as Mexico Park.

Quinceaños in Mexico Park
A young lady poses for a photographer before her fifteenth birthday party at the edge of Mexico Park. [Sevilla Metro, eight blocks southeast]

Clock in Mexico Park
Reflecting the deco style popular in the Condessa neighborhood, the clock is a popular meeting place.

Stew Pots
Prepared food sold at the *tianguis* is inexpensive and delicious.

Lindbergh Theater
Designed by Roberto Montenegro, this stage in Mexico Park honors Charles Lindbergh, who spent some time here. It is often used for community events.

Woman with Water Jugs
This fountain stands outside the Lindbergh Theater.

Lincoln Park

In the Polanco neighborhood, Lincoln Park is a heavily used recreation area. This statue of Lincoln donated by the American Embassy stands directly across from one of Martin Luther King, Jr. [Auditorio Metro, three blocks north, three blocks west]

Shady Benches in Lincoln Park

The shaded reflecting pools and many benches make this a comfortable park for strolling or sitting. On Sundays the pools are filled with remote controlled model boats.

Saturday Market

On Saturdays, vendors sell fresh fruits and vegetables in Lincoln Park. These markets, known as *tianguis,* are traditional Indian roaming markets begun in pre-Columbian times.

Clockwise from top:

Uruguay Plaza
The city of Montevideo, Uruguay, donated a bronze statue of General Josè Artigas to the city and the plaza was completed with a cubist style fountain. Locals relax during the lunch hour in the Polanco neighborhood. [Polanco Metro, four blocks east]

Plaza Melchor Campo
Tightly pruned boxwood surround a fountain in the middle of this busy traffic circle. [Metro Sevilla, seven blocks northeast]

Peace Plaza
Peace Plaza pavilion in Tlatelolco is used for concerts, meetings, and exercising. [Tlatelolco Metro stop, three blocks north]

Plaza Juaregui
This shady plaza is surrounded by the buildings of Pan American University, Simon Bolivar University, and a church. [Metro stop Mixcoac, six blocks east, three blocks south]

Parque Hundido
Hundido means "Big Hole," the local name for Louis Urbide Park, which was once a clay source for nearby brickyards. The leftover hole is now an interesting park. The flag of Mexico flies over a floral clock. [Parque Hundido Metrobus stop]

Iztapalapa Park
Bright stainless steel sculptures have Aztec themes alongside the Virgin of Guadalupe. [Iztapalapa Metro stop, two blocks north]

Garden Path in Casa de la Bola
Paths throughout the garden behind this opulent colonial mansion in Lira Park create a cool maze in which to get lost. [Tacubaya Metro stop, four blocks northwest]

50 Years of Rock and Roll
In the Roman Lopez Velarde Garden, fifty top Mexican rock and roll bands from the years 1956 to 2006 are memorialized. [Directly west of Centro Medico Metro stop]

Opposite:
Casa de la Bola Gardens
The gardens behind Casa de la Bola are adorned with classical sculptures and fountains.

[Take Metro to Universidad. The university has its own busses with routes through the campus.]

IN 2007 THIS HUGE SITE, known as University City, was added to UNESCO's World Heritage list. Some of its buildings are, in effect, murals. These buildings, botanical gardens, an outstanding sculpture collection, and three excellent museums, make the campus a work of art worth visiting. Buildings constructed from 1949-1954 provide backgrounds for mammoth mosaic works of art. Important Mexican muralists such as David Alfaro Siqueiros, Diego Rivera, Francisco Eppens, and Juan O'Gorman have designed the exterior faces of several buildings. The more than 50-year-old, mature botanical gardens feature a complete selection of tropical arid zone plantings with excellent identification (in Spanish and Latin). Greenhouses contain a great variety of tropical jungle species in natural arrangement. In addition, a 363-acre ecological preserve was established in 1983 and includes an impressive sculptural space within its boundaries.

In 1979, the University president, Guillermo Soberón, asked six prominent Mexican sculptors, Helen Escobedo, Sebastián, Mathias Goeritz, Hersúa, Federico Silva, and Manuel Felgeruez, to fill the space around the new buildings of UNAM's cultural center with sculpture. The sculptors asked the various academics at the university for ideas about the design for the space. The botanists wanted to preserve the desert plants, the geologists asked to expose the volcanic rock on which the university sits, and anthropologists said they were sure there were pre-Columbian remains under the rock. The unusual collaborative result, Sculptural Space I, blends all three disciplines. Sixty-four pentahedral buttresses in a circular layout 394 feet in diameter are reminiscent of early pre-Columbian astronomical ceremonial sites. They surround a sea of lava and rest in an area of native plants. This impressive circular sculpture sits at the edge of the ecological preserve. In Sculptural Space II, centered in the university's cultural center across the street, each artist has contributed a large scale individual piece. Growing out of a vast, volcanic bowl of natural vegetation, the large sculptures take on an organic presence. Walking among the buildings, gardens, and sculptures of UNAM invokes a feeling of magical transformation in time and space.

Central Library
Ten stories high, with murals by Juan O'Gorman, Gustavo Saavedra, and Jaun Martìnez de Velasco on all sides, this is the largest mosaic in the world. Finished in 1950, the murals narrate 400 years of Mexican history.

UNIVERSIDAD NACIONAL AUTÓNOMA DE MÉXICO (UNAM)

UNIVERSIDAD NACIONAL D MEXICO

Allegory of Culture
This side wall of the rectory tower on campus features the dates of the Mexican peoples' greatest struggles in a 1952 mosaic mural by David Alfaro Siqueros.

University for the People
The north face of the rectory tower depicts the social function of the university in Siqueros' mural.

Antonio Caso Auditorium
A 1992 mosaic mural by Chavez Morado depicts the myth of Prometheus on the side of the auditorium.

Tlaloc
This sculpture, created by Sebastiàn in 1980, is named for the Aztec rain god.

Kepler's Key
Manuel Felguèrez's sculpture (1980) sits near the education buildings.

Coatl
By Helen Escobedo (1980), this piece invites interaction. Not only have people written on this and other sculptures, but they also enjoy climbing on them.

Colotl
Sebastiàn's sculpture, *Scorpion*, sits like a folded piece of paper.

Opposite:

Sculptural Space II
Contemporary sculpture is viewed in the valley of rocky, volcanic soil ringed by UNAM's modern buildings.

Crown of the Pedregal
The bright pink towers, sculpted by Matìas Goeritz in 1980, thrust out of the volcanic rocks and soil called the *pedregal*.

Serpents of the Pedregal
Created by Federico Silva in 1986, this long, snaking wall-like structure defines one side of Sculptural Space II at UNAM.

Serpents of the Pedregal Gates
Centered in the sculpture that forms the wall are gates to Sculptural Space II.

Opposite:
Aves Dos
The massive *Two Birds*, by Hersùa (1980), sits in the volcanic landscape.

Sculptural Space
Designed by Matìas Goeritz, a series of 64 giant buttresses combine a futuristic concept with strong traditions. It has features of the Aztec calendar, as well as the cosmic view of the pre-Columbian world.

Helio Bravo Botanical Garden
Century plants spear toward the sun and prepare to bloom, surrounded by a natural looking arid zone landscape. The Botany Department of UNAM performs important plant research here.

Mature Cacti
A huge agave in the foreground and old yucca in the background attest to the maturity of the garden, which was moved from Chapultepec Park in 1959.

Clumps of Agave
Cat ear (Aeonium undatam) grows wild in Mexico and hangs from ledges. It is at home in UNAM's rocky volcanic soil.

Climbing Tiger Paws
Tiger paws climb the two-story wall of the greenhouse in UNAM's gardens.

Huge Lobster Claw
The flowers of this lobster claw are close to two feet long.

Jungle Greenhouse
The Manuel Ruiz Oronoz Greenhouse has an excellent collection of tropical plants indigenous to Mexico's jungles. Spider lilies (Hymenocallis x macrostephana), lobster claw (Heliconia), and tiger paws (Monstera deliciosa araceae) grow along tiered stone walkways.

Banana Leaf
Large native banana plants (Ensete) glow with sun in the UNAM greenhouse.

Flowering Aloe
Kranz aloe (Aloe arborescens) grows well and flowers in the dry, sunny climate at UNAM.

San Ángel Façade
The wall of a house across from Archangel Square in San Ángel is covered with bougainvillea.

AS THE SPREADING MEGAPOLIS BEGAN to engulf small colonial neighborhoods in the nineteenth and twentieth centuries, old adobe and stone houses were destroyed to build large, modern condominiums and office buildings. In most cases, all that remains of an old neighborhood is a church and a public square. A few of these neighborhoods have managed to hold on to their colonial charm and are prestigious places in which to live. These include Coyoacán, San Angel, and Tlapan. All three have expanded from their charming central squares to modern shopping malls and buildings, but the old historic areas are worth a visit.

The Indian village of Coyoacan, a Náhuatl word meaning "Place of Coyotes," became one of the bases of operation for Cortés after the fall of Tenochtitlán. The shores of Lake Texcoco extended up to it at the time of the Spanish conquest. Its narrow cobbled streets and colonial plazas retain their provincial charm. It held the honor of being the fifth most livable neighborhood in North America according to a 2004 survey by the Project on Public Spaces.

San Ángel and Chimalistac were once suburbs where the aristocracy from Mexico City kept summer residences. They were built among huge orchards managed by Carmelite monks and a large *pulque* hacienda where agave, used to make the fermented drink, was grown. Today they are picturesque residential neighborhoods with cobblestone streets lined with colonial homes and modern homes that compliment colonial style. Gardens and small, shady plazas are scattered throughout the area.

Further south in the city, Tlapan, Náhuatl for "Place of Solid Ground," has been populated since 1200 B.C. Volcanic eruptions drove the early inhabitants out of the area by the fourth century. In the sixteenth century it was part of the Valley of Oaxaca Marquisate owned by Hernán Cortés. By the seventeenth century it had its own governor and, a day trip away from the center of Mexico City, had become a recreational area for city residents. In 1827 it was the capital of the state of Mexico and was incorporated into Mexico City in 1855. It is the largest *delegación* and spreads over most of the southern part of the city. Its main square, with a baroque church founded by Dominican friars in 1547, stands as it did then. Cobblestone streets with seventeenth and eighteenth century buildings fan out from the the square

The colonial centers of these neighborhoods retain their own vibrant identities amidst a modern, urbane city. Each also hosts at least one museum, a market, a community center, and several parks.

COLONIAL NEIGHBORHOODS

Nº6B

Opposite:

Church Arcade

Founded in 1547, the Church of San Agustin de las Cuevas in Tlapan retains the arcades of its cloisters. [To old Tlapan, take the Tren Ligero to Estadio Azteca, then a taxi to the Plaza la Paz]

San Agustin de las Cuevas

Built in baroque style, the church still serves the neighborhood of Tlapan as it has since the sixteenth century.

Del Carmen Courtyard in San Ángel

Thick stone walls and interior fresco paintings preserve the atmosphere in this San Ángel church and convent, where Carmelite monks lived and tended fruit trees. [Metrobus stop La Bombilla, taxi to Del Carmen or San Jacinto Square]

Underpass Mural
Murals abound in Mexico City. This one painted on the sides of an underpass leading into Tlapan has a clear message.

Church Archway
Decorated for a confirmation ceremony, baby's breath and white roses form an arch over the door to the church of San Jacinto in San Ángel.

Atrium Wall
Bougainvillea (Nyctaginaceae) climb over the walls, surrounding the atrium of San Jacinto.

Saturday Bazaar
Artists set up and line San Jacinto Plaza on Saturdays in San Ángel.

Opposite:
Guadalupe Altar
This altar to the Virgin of Guadalupe sits at the edge of San Jacinto Plaza.

Archangel Square
Violet jacaranda trees, intense purple and red bougainvillea, bananas, and azaleas densely fill this tiny square tucked into a San Ángel neighborhood.

Garden of Art
Boxes with pruned azaleas, ferns, and kaffir lilies adorn this garden at the edge of San Ángel.

Bridge over No Water
In the seventeenth century, three bridges crossed the Magdalena River, which flowed out of the mountains. Now diverted into pipes, the river leaves behind the bridges along the Magdalena River Walk in Chimalistac, a residential neighborhood close to San Ángel. [Metrobus to La Bombilla, taxi to Magdalena River Walk]

Cactus Fence
Organ-pipe cactus (Pachycereus marginatus) form a fence in front of the Diego Rivera house in San Ángel. [Metrobus to La Bombilla, taxi to Diego Rivera House]

Tagle Park
Mature yuccas find a bit of sun in this shady, peaceful park in Chimalistac. [Metrobus to La Bombilla, two blocks southeast]

Clockwise from top:

St. John the Baptist Church in Centenario Park
Construction of this church and convent in Coyoacán began in the sixteenth century—it is one of the oldest churches in central Mexico.

Organ Grinder
The hand of the organ grinder in Centenario Park is a blur while he tirelessly pumps the hand organ. He lives on tips from appreciative audiences. Organ grinders are found in tourist spots throughout the city.

Centenario Park
Old archways to what was once the church atrium mark the entrance to this park in Coyoacán. On weekends the park is filled with vendors. [Metro to Viveros, taxi to Centenario Park]

Old Ornamentation
The Chapel of St. Anthony Panzacola in the historic section of Coyoacán is decorated with a common spiral motif. [Metro to Viveros, taxi to Avenida Francisco Sosa]

Hidalgo Hedges
Boxwood hedges in the Hidalgo Park gardens are closely pruned into spirals. Wormwood (Artemisia) provides color contrast.

Hidalgo Park
In Hidalgo Park, next to St. John the Baptist Church, bougainvillea climbs a cedar tree. In season, roses bloom in the center of circular boxwood hedges. [Metro to Viveros, taxi to Hidalgo Park]

Chapel of St. Catherine
This chapel sits on Francisco Sosa Street, which retains its colonial charm in the historic section of Coyoacán.

Opposite:
Side Street
Francisco Sosa Street in Coyoacán is an old cobblestone street with colorful colonial homes. This is one of its narrow side streets. [Metro to Viveros, taxi to Avenida Francisco Sosa]

Patio Wall
The walls of Frida Kahlo's "Blue House" in Coyoacán are imbedded with shells and pottery to set off her collection of pre-Columbian sculpture. [Metro to Viveros, taxi to Casa de Frida Kahlo]

Opposite:

Tending Seedlings
One of several workers weeds small seedlings. The Viveros Gardens in Coyoacán are one of two areas in the city that propagate and grow plants for the city's parks.

Viveros Avenue
Circled by a well-used running/walking track with kilometer markers, the Viveros Gardens in Coyoacán are crossed by several pedestrian avenues such as this one. [Metro to Viveros]

Coyote Guards
The neighborhood of Coyoacán has several coyote statues guarding its boundaries. This one is located near the Miguel Angel de Quevedo subway stop. Coyoacán means "Place of Coyotes" in Nàhuatl. [Metro Miguel Angel de Quevedo]

The Route of Friendship

[Metrobus to Perisur, then take a taxi to Cuemanco. Huge sculptures line the southern Periferico, Mexico City's beltway.]

RUTA DE AMISTAD TURNED OUT TO BE an ironic name for part of the Periferico, a ten-and-one-half-mile stretch of Mexico City's outer beltway, which was lined with mammoth sculptures to welcome participants and observers to the city for the 1968 Olympics. A week prior to the opening ceremonies, on October 2, a massacre of close to 400 protestors by police occurred. It was during the time of student protests in Paris, the Kent State massacre, and the Chicago Seven protests in the United States. Students in Mexico City joined the climate of unrest and organized a demonstration in Tlatelolco's Plaza of Three Cultures. They were protesting single-party rule and restricted freedom of speech. They had been protesting for months. President Gustavo Díaz Ordaz (1964-70) was known for his authoritarian style. This was the first time the Olympics were set in a developing nation and he was anxious for Mexico to appear stable to the rest of the world. During the demonstration of October 2, the area was cordoned off by the police, tanks were nearby and helicopters hovered overhead. A flare was dropped from one of the helicopters and shots rang out from a balcony where speakers stood. Authorities say that students fired the first shots and the demonstrators say the police opened fire. In either case, although the government reported only twenty deaths, the number was actually closer to 400. The truthful details of the massacre have never been uncovered, in spite of an investigation by President Vicente Fox's administration (2000-2004).

Díaz attempted to minimize the extent of the confrontation until after the Olympics. Skeptical Mexicans have little hope that the truth will ever come to light. The Plaza of Three Cultures remains as a monument to the dead and the giant, colorful sculptures along the Route of Friendship now lead to deteriorating Olympic sites.

The Periferico sculpture garden was the brainchild of Mattius Goerritz, a well-known Mexican sculptor who worked in the 1950s and 1960s designing buildings and huge public sculptures. His Sculptural Space I at UNAM and mammoth skyscraper shapes at Cuidad Satèlite on the other end of the beltway are landmarks in the city. Artists from countries all over the world were invited to create giant cement sculptures to decorate the approach to the Olympic sporting facilities that were built along the southern end of the city. Goerritz carefully controlled the size and design, placing them at intervals in the line of sight as one drives or rides along the super highway. Goerritz's vision of art on a grand scale helps make this city unique.

Fallen Comrades
Some twenty names are listed to memorialize the nearly 400 protestors killed in 1968 in the Plaza of Three Cultures. Fiberglass casts of this monument are found on the campus of UNAM, the university which many of the protestors attended.

Opposite:
Plaza of Three Cultures
The vast plaza has a forlorn feeling as if to testify to its bloody history.

Señales
Signals, by Angela Guerrìa of Mexico, is the first of the mammoth sculptures beside the beltway in the southern part of the city.

Opposite:
El Ancla
Like a disassembled puzzle, the tail of *The Anchor*, by Willi Gutmann of Switzerland, seems to anchor this large disk and keep it from rolling into traffic.

Nesquik
BOLT
PEMEX
PEMEX
3335

Esferas
These striking, bisected *Spheres,* by Kioshi Takahashi of Japan, sit near the huge studios of TV Azteca.

Las Tres Graces
Brightly painted, *The Three Graces*, by Miloslav Chiupac of Czechoslavakia, loom over the busy beltway.

El Sol Bipedo
Near a new shopping mall, this piece sits in a little park dotted with spheres that echo the design of the small balls surrounding the *Two Legged Sun* by Pierre Szekely of France.

Reloj Solar

Grzegorz Kowalski of Poland created *Solar Clock* placed near the intersection of the Periferico and Insurgentes Avenue.

Untitled, Italy

Using the colors of the Italian flag, Constantino Nivola of Italy places a bird atop the strong base. This piece sits in the area known as the pedregal, where volcanic rock from a pre-Columbian eruption is the predominant feature of the soil.

Torre del Viento
Tower of the Wind, by Gonzalo Fanseca of Uruguay, is the only sculpture that can be entered. It sometimes hosts events inside and around it.

Mexico
By Jose Maria Subirachs of Spain, the Olympic ring-like circles become part of the strong triangular motif of this piece.

Untitled, Belgium
Visible from the highway, this piece by Jacques Moeschal of Belgium sits behind a chain link fence with barbed wire. The piece seems to stand guard over the ruins of the pre-Columbian Cuicuilco culture, as well as the Olympic stadium.

Untitled, USA
This sculpture by Todd Williams is surrounded by the original Olympic venues, which are now part of a sports club.

Muro Articulado

Articulated Wall, by Herbert Bayer of Austria, is seen from the windows of one of hundreds of busses that circumnavigate the city on the Periferico each day.

Opposite:

Tertulia de Gigante

By Joop J. Beljon of Holland, *Meeting of the Giants* was freshly painted but already tagged with graffiti. The open accessibility of the pieces makes them easy targets for graffiti artists.

Sol Rojo

Red Sun, by Alexander Calder, blazes in front of the Aztec Stadium. Built just before the Olympics, the stadium now hosts soccer competitions.

EL SAMO

Untitled, France
By Oliver Seguin of France, like most of the sculptures on the Periferico, this piece provides a surface for graffiti. The city paints the pieces regularly.

Opposite:

Untitled, Australia
Protected by a locked fence, this piece by Clement Meadmore of Australia sits on the grounds of a private school.

MEGANE Sedan
$16,975
ENGANCHE

Opposite:

Puerta de Paz
When he named this piece *Door of Peace,* Itzhak Danziger of Israel had no idea of the brutal massacre that would precede the Olympics in 1968.

Puerto al Viento
Door to the Wind, by Helen Escobedo of Mexico, seems to move—a feat unusual among the large cement sculptures.

Untitled, Morocco
Undulating like the busy, nearby traffic cloverleaf, this piece by Mohamed Melchi of Morocco seems to be secured to the median strip by its red, steel fence.

Cuemanco Channel
A viewing stand, stadium seats, and flagpoles remain at the Olympic rowing venue. This site is used by runners and rowers, as well as athletes who use the exercise equipment near the stands.

Opposite:
Untitled, Mexico
These two pieces by Jorge Dubon of Mexico stand outside the Cuemanco Channel, which was built for the Olympic rowing competitions.

No Se Olvida
"Never Forget" posters and exhibits remind citizens of Mexico City to never forget the events of October 2, 1968. The huge sculptures lining the southern beltway of the city stand like monuments to the fallen.

[To reach the Basilica complex, take the Metro to La Villa Basilica, walk two blocks north.]

TO TRULY UNDERSTAND the Mexican spirit, one must visit this complex of cathedrals, chapels, and monuments to the only two Mexican saints, the Virgin of Guadalupe and Saint Juan Diego. In the northern region of the city, Tepeyac, the hill on which the miracles occurred, also happens to have been the site of a temple to Tonantzin, an Aztec goddess. In 1531, the legend tells us, Juan Diego, a recent convert to Catholicism, saw a vision of a beautiful, dark-skinned virgin surrounded by light. She ordered him to have a chapel built in her honor. The Bishop did not believe Juan Diego—even after two more visions. At last she provided proof. She filled Diego's cape with roses and imprinted her image upon it. When the church fathers saw this tangible proof, they went about building the first chapel on the hill where she had appeared. Since then, two more cathedrals, a convent, a baptismal, a chapel dedicated to Saint Juan Diego, and a small chapel over a spring that she is said to have made appear have been built. The Basílica attracts millions of pilgrims annually, many crawling the last several hundred feet on their knees. The Virgin of Guadalupe is ever present throughout the country, which is 90% Catholic. Small shrines to her are tucked into corners of parks, subway stations, and neighborhoods. Her image everywhere serves as a daily reminder of the special customs of Mexican Catholicism.

BASÍLICA DE GUADALUPE

Opposite:

St. Michael

Archangel St. Michael guards the old chapel on Tepeyac Hill.

Basílicas Old and New

The modern Basílica, built in 1976, was designed to look like a cape. The old Basílica, completed in the sixteenth century, stands in the middle with the Capuchin nun's convent beside it.

Festival of the Virgin
From December 6 to 12, the days of the miraculous appearance of Guadalupe, pilgrims come to honor her. They let helium balloons rise into the air and sing to call her.

Atrium Cross
A sundial on the south side, Aztec calendar on the north, clock on the east, and a carillon on the west represent man's measurement of time. The carillon opens up every hour and mechanized figures reenact the apparitions of Juan Diego. The bells call the faithful to mass.

Floral Offering
Built on elaborate straw and plaster frames, flower offerings are brought to the Basílica from parishes all over the country. This one over the front doors of the new Basílica is from one of Mexico City's suburbs, Iztapalapa.

New Basílica Altar
Mass is offered several times a day during the Festival of Guadalupe.

Moving Walkway
Juan Diego's original cape featuring the image of Guadalupe is kept in a highly secure case that pilgrims can view from a moving walkway that goes behind the altar. The image is visible from anywhere inside the Basílica.

John Paul II
The statue stands in front of the Popemobile used in each of the Pope's four visits to Mexico. Pilgrims, who will stay until December 12, rest with their camping gear.

Pilgrims
People come from all over Mexico bringing their images of the Virgin and Juan Diego to be blessed by the priests. They kneel in front of the Basílica and sing songs blessing Guadalupe.

Viejitos
"Old Ones" dance in front of the Basílica. Pre-Columbian in origin, dancers hobble around with canes and sometimes fall over. This group does a rhythmic tap dance and follows two pretty señoritas around. Various dancers arrive all year, including Concheros and Chinelos.

1531
DEL
2008

Opposite:

Souvenir

Photographers offering colorful souvenir photos line the approach to Tepeyac Hill, where Juan Diego had his visions.

Pilgrims Approach the Basílica

Early in the morning, crowds of people begin to file into the square in front of the Basílica.

Tepeyac Chapel
Indians visit this chapel on Tepeyac Hill, or the Little Hill.

Offerings
A Catholic priest and Indians bring offerings to Guadalupe in this sculpture on Tepeyac. Roses planted in the foreground remind one of the miracle.

Jaguar Fountains
Many of the early Aztec symbols, such as the jaguar, a fierce warrior group, can be found among the European Catholic images.

Vision with Roses
The site of one of Juan Diego's visions is marked by this sculpture of him showing his robe to the bishop.

Opposite:

Conch Shell Blowers

As the Cardinal and the procession of bishops enter the atrium of the Chapel of Juan Diego, conch shells are blown to announce the beginning of the mass. This is a pre-Columbian Indian tradition.

Fortune Teller

At the base of the Little Hill are winged fortune tellers. For a few pesos, trained birds come out of their cages, do some tricks like put the hat on the doll, then pluck a fortune for you out of the box to the left.

Conch

In the fountain at the base of the hill sits a conch shell, an important religious symbol for the Aztec. Conches are blown to summon the gods.

Opposite:

Holy Ghost

The gilded ceiling of the Chapel of Juan Diego radiates.

Mother and Child

This Indian mother has dressed her baby with an image of Guadalupe on his shirt. They stand in front of the altar of the Chapel of Juan Diego. She wears the hairy wool skirt worn in the state of Chiapas.

Broadcasting the Message

As the Cardinal directs the mass, a woman holds her cell phone up to the speaker.

EL AZTEQUITA

Opposite:

Aztequitas

Followers of an indigenous branch of the Catholic Church leave the mass conducted at the Chapel of San Diego.

St. Jude

St. Jude, patron saint of lost causes, stands in the Chapel of the Little Well with images of people requesting his intervention attached to his cloak. This chapel marks the spot where Guadalupe is said to have made a well miraculously appear.

Wheat Vendor

Colorful sprigs of wheat with religious images attached are sold near the Basílica.

[To Xochimilco, take the Tren Ligero to the end at the Xochimilco stop. Taxi or ask one of the many guides on bikes to take you to the boats or the church.]

Tranijera
A freshly painted boat sits drying so that the table and chairs can be placed in it. The color scheme is *alegra*, or happy.

XOCHIMILCO IS AN NÁHUATL WORD meaning, "The Place Where Flowers are Grown." The magic of this place evolved from a long tradition that originated in pre-Columbian times. When Cortès and his army conquered Tenochtitlán, later named Mexico City, it was an island in a lake with a vast network of canals. The Canals at Xochimilco, twelve and one-half miles south of the city center, were left alone to provide food for the conquerors and the Spanish began to fill in the lake and canals where the center of the city sits today. The traditional *chinampas*, floating gardens, still exist and are farmed in much the same way as in pre-Columbian times. To create *chinampas*, ahuejote trees (tall poplars) anchored woven mats that were covered with muck from the shallow canals.

These rich fields are still tended by people of Indian descent who travel in flat-bottomed boats and canoes from their houses in the neighborhoods, or *barrios*. Much of the produce today is ornamental. Thousands of potted marigolds are grown for the Days of the Dead at the end of October, poinsettias for the Christmas season, and lilies for the Easter season.

Declared a World Heritage Site by UNESCO in 1987, the area has been a popular tourist spot since the 1920s. A colorful flat-bottomed *tranijera* with a long table and chairs can be rented by the hour and poled through the water lily choked canals. The Xochimilco Ecological Park, completed in 1993, does not allow vendors and is a serene, excellent site for bird watching. There is a visitor center and boats and bikes can be rented to explore the 300-acre site. Other canals are populated by vendors in boats selling food, drink, jewelry, or musical entertainment. The canals are home to the endangered axolotl, a salamander, and it is possible to visit rescue operations.

The colonia has a fascinating religious custom. A baby Christ, or Niñopan, is kept by one family for a year and keeping a special room for him and his cupboards of toys and clothing is part of the responsibility. This 200-year-old doll goes to church every day and visits sick and needy parishioners over the year. He wears his doctor outfit when he visits the ill. The job of caring for him and taking him to appointments is full time and families are signed up for this honor for the next 80 years. A festival in honor of the change of the family is held every Candlemas in February at the Cathedral of San Bernadino.

Whether gliding through Xochimilco's canals to enjoy nature or to experience the festivities, it promises to be an unforgettable experience.

XOCHIMILCO

Cathedral of San Bernadino
The church was completed in 1590 and Franciscan monks founded a school where the Náhuatl language of the Aztec was taught.

Niñopan
Every year on Candlemas, February 2, this icon is turned over to a new family for safekeeping in their home. He is the center of a cult that worships baby Jesus in *barrios* all over the city.

Niñopan Goes Home
A Niñopan doll is paraded through the streets to the barrio where he lives. Chinelo dancers lead the way and keep the crowd back.

OPTIC
15 AÑOS

Opposite:

Chinelos

In the late 1800s, Indians in the state of Morelos dressed in costume as Spaniards to dance anonymously in the Carnival parade. Chinelo dancers twirl and dance to a brass band at various celebrations in the city.

Xochimilco Canal

The canals of Xochimilco are called the "Venice of the Western Hemisphere."

Chinelo

Practice begins at an early age and it is an honor to become a Chinelo dancer.

Tourist Zone
This part of the main canal is busy with vendors selling food, drink, handicrafts, and musical entertainment.

Tranijeras
Hundreds of *tranijeras* named after women and saints line the canals of Xochimilco to provide rides for tourists and locals. At one time the arch was decorated with real flowers but now it's plaster of Paris over straw.

Opposite:
Mariachi Boat
For a small fee, the mariachi band will tie up to your boat and serenade your group.

XOCHIMILCO

Opposite:

Trajinerador with Mascota
Poling up and down the canals in the morning are people on their way to work their *chinampas*, or fields. Notice the hoe, rake, and scythe in the back of the boat.

Clockwise from top:

Isla de las Muñecas
Don Julian farmed and created a memorial to a little girl who drowned near his *chinampa*. Although he has died, the island still memorializes him and the girl.

Chinampa
Ajuehote, a type of tall poplar, provides roots for the muck that is built up from the canals to create fertile fields like those farmed in the same way by Indians thousands of years ago. Corn is growing on this island.

Ecological Park Visitor Center
The roof of the visitor center at the park provides a view of the surrounding Sierra Nevada Mountains and the barrios of Xochimilco.

Park Canal
New canals were dug in the park to connect it to the historic *chinampa* area. The Sierra Nevada Mountains and volcanoes are in the background. Vendors are not allowed in the Ecological Zone.

Walkway Pergola
An armature for climbing vines and beds of demonstration flower gardens frame an entry to the Ecological Zone.

Xochimilco Park Flower Market
The Ecological Park includes a large 1800 stall flower market selling seasonal flowers.

Dry Docked
Rowboats are stacked during the winter season while the lake in Bosque de Aragon is cleaned.

MEXICO CITY HAS A DEPARTMENT of the Environment, which seems to take the need for spacious green areas seriously. This department provides oxygen via trees and other vegetation, as well as space for its citizens to escape the concrete. The areas that provide water for the city are off limits for development, as well. The huge Valley of Mexico is not completely filled with houses and tall buildings. At its southernmost border are found thousands of acres of green forested areas that have been declared national parks or city Ecological Zones. The vast wild areas south of the city are like strong shoulders upon which the bustling city rests its head. These areas are visited by citizens of Mexico City on weekends in particular. At the northern edges are smaller protected areas. The northern zone is strikingly different from the southern and few people walk in the dry, arid hills there. Southwest of the city is the edge of the Sierra de las Cruces mountain range and a gateway into areas that have been popular for cooler climes and recreation for generations. Within the city limits one can also find steep extinct volcanoes that have been protected and are now used for recreation. In 1988 several pieces of undeveloped land on each edge of the city were set aside for recreation. Most of these contain vestiges of Lake Texcoco, the vast lake in which the Aztecs had built their big city, Tenochtitlán. After European colonization, the shallow lake was gradually filled and the city spread out over thirty miles in every direction before city leaders felt a need to preserve some of the undeveloped land and canals. Even without a vehicle, one can escape by bus or subway to an area that is green and forested in Mexico City.

PARKS ON THE EDGE

Opposite:

Bosque de Aragon

The *bosque*, or woods, of this park is a young forest. [Metro stop Bosque de Aragon lets you out in front of the park.]

Clockwise from top:

Aragon Lake

Boats are rented by the hour to row around in this park located on the northeast edge of the city.

Tenochtitlàn Island

In Tezomoc Park, in the northwest corner of the city, a replica of the statue in the Historic District that depicts the Mexica Indians discovering the site that became Mexico City is surrounded by bright columns representing other Indian tribes that lived in the valley when the Spanish arrived. [Metro stop El Rosario, taxi to Tezomoc Park]

Aragon Sculpture

Tall sculptures throughout the park seem to grow out of the ground.

Opposite:

Boxers

After roping off a boxing ring, men practice their skills in the park.

Alameda Oriente Cactus Garden

This healthy cactus garden is nurtured by compost made on site. The agaves are about ready to bloom.

Orange Sedum

Colorful succulents like these sedum blanket the landscape at the zoo.

Zoo Planting

Arid zone plants like this sotol compliment the menagerie in the Aragon Park Zoo.

Alameda Oriente Palapas

This park on the eastern edge of the city is next to the airport. Mature cycads (Cycadaceae) provide greenery and the roofed *palapas* provide shade for gatherings. [Metro stop Pantitlan, taxi to Alameda Oriente]

Alameda Oriente Open Air Theater
A mural depicts the modernization of the city next to a stage used for community events.

Tepeyac National Park
North of the city, the dry forest climate of this land set aside for recreational use is not as popular for leisure activities as the parks on the southern boundaries. [Metro to Villa la Basílica, taxi to Tepeyac Park]

Ducks on the Lake
Boats are rented at the lake of Bosque de Tlahauc in the southeast corner of the city. A track around the lake is popular with runners and walkers. [Tren Ligero to Periferico, bus to Cuemanco, bus to Tlahauc.]

Clockwise from top:

Tlahauc Exercisers
A group of athletes works out on the track in Bosque de Tlahauc. This park has two tracks, a lake, a community center, arts center, and an ice skating rink.

Park Shelter
Bosque de Tlapan is full of stone and log shelters for picnickers.

Bubbling Brook
At the edge of Tlapan, water trucks line up and wait their turn to fill up with the fresh mountain water that runs through a lake feeding a brook in Fuentes Brotantes Park. The water is pumped from a pumping station and used to irrigate green space all over the neighborhood. It rarely rains in the city from October to April and park vegetation needs frequent watering. [Metrobus to Fuentes Brotantes]

Runners in Tlapan
In the Tlapan *bosque*, or forest, located on the southern edge of the city, nearby schools and locals have several running tracks they can use. [Metrobus to Ayuntamiento, four blocks west]

Convent of Desierto de los Leones
In the early seventeenth century, Carmelite monks founded this remote monastery about 30 miles southwest of the center of the city. The name *Desierto,* or "Desert," was related to the idea that the monks were isolated like Jesus in the desert. Leones refers to the family who owned the land where the convent is located. [Metrobus to Perisur, taxi to Desierto de los Leones Park]

Convent Grounds
Beautifully landscaped grounds are now visited by hundreds of people each week. This walkway runs from the convent to a chapel. The Carmelites left the convent in 1780.

Acanthus
Imported from Europe, the acanthus (Acanthaceae) is a popular, easy to grow ornamental in Mexico City parks.

Convent Garden
Roses grow inside the tightly pruned boxwood along the convent wall.

Opposite:

Desierto de los Leones Forest

The nearby forest provides a cool, fragrant escape for city dwellers and features 4613 acres of oak, cedar, and fir trees. Established in 1917, this is Mexico's first national park although it is within the city limits.

Cliffs of Dinamos

At the city's southern border, Parque Nacional de los Dinamos is popular with rock climbers. It once provided water for hydroelectric plants on the Magdalena Contreras River, which runs down the middle of the canyon. A now defunct cotton thread plant in a village at the edge of the canyon used generators at the power plant for electricity. [Metrobus to Perisur, taxi to Dinamos Park]

Ajusco Park

The approach to Ajusco Park, another southern mountain park, is populated by cattle ranches that also offer horseback riding. [Metrobus to Perisur, taxi to Ajusco Park]

Forests of Ajusco
Xitle volcano rises 7217 feet in the distance as one approaches the city limits. Last erupting in 1719, this is one of at least fourteen volcanoes within the city limits.

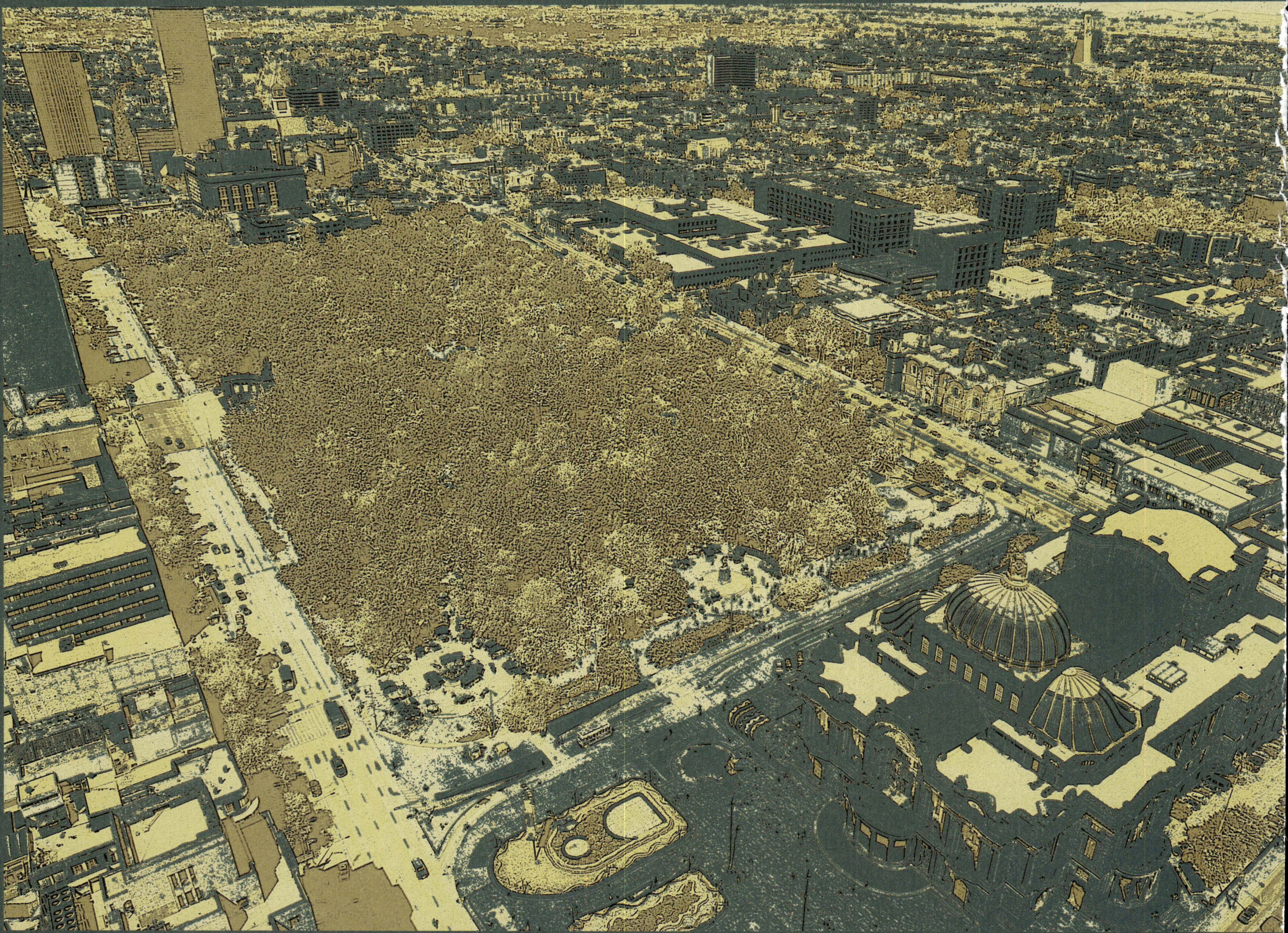